Wet Reckless

Cassandra Dallett

Manic D Press
San Francisco

For Chopper, Rosie, and Rae

Wet Reckless ©2014 by Cassandra Dallet. All rights reserved.
Published by Manic D Press. For information, contact Manic D Press,
PO Box 410804, San Francisco CA 94141   www.manicdpress.com

ISBN 978-1-933149-84-4   Printed in the USA

*Wet Reckless is a nickname for the California Vehicle Code (VC) Section 23103.5 statute of reckless driving involving alcohol. If the prosecutor assesses that a DUI case has some weaknesses — for example, when a breath or blood test result is close to the .08 legal limit, and if the arresting officer's assessment of driving and Field Sobriety Tests are inconclusive — the prosecutor might offer a plea bargain ... a Wet Reckless.

Contents

I come from Mud Pond
murky under its tangle of lily pads
dirty kitchen of smoke from wood stove and weed.

I come from Fillmore
how it was before highrises
flat lands stretched behind chain link
razed tenements, old men with watermelon trucks
and the 22 right on through.

I come from Richmond
by the tracks concrete and steel
our little piece of peace
wedged into its iron point.

I come from Oakland
where roosters and crows talk
from the back of the house
to gunshots and stereos in the front,
where I'm afraid to turn on the local bad news
but grow succulent roots in clay soil and
find home.

'69

I was almost born at Woodstock
but when the freak scene stumbled
from around our kitchen table
and drifted off towards upstate NY,
my pregnant parents sunk into
the quiet wake left behind
and stayed in Vermont.

They drove up and over Old City Falls Road
to Barbara and Syd's house
sat around their table between
brightly painted doors,
hand thrown pots,
and the smell of rotting food.

Under blackening skies
they tuned up the old radio
to listen to the concert.
Barbara went on one of her trips
ranting about the static
when a karmic bolt of lighting
hit the radio.

Woodstock went up in a tiny mushroom cloud.

Buying the Mountain

Tiger lilies freckled stone cellar holes
orange as Krishna robes
apple tree blossoms
a sweet orchard on top of the world

None of them bloomed after we moved in
and the apples were all crab

Swimming Whole

I was a hippie child dirty and wild
feet sinking into brown soil in my mother's garden.
Squeezing mud through my toes in the duck pond
running fast across burning asphalt in front of the village store.

The screen door slamming behind me
across the creaking wood floor, squinting in the dimly lit interior
to place an orange Creamsicle on the dingy counter
between the tall jars of pickled eggs and sausages.

Back to the hot cracked vinyl backseat.
My feet making familiar music of glass beer bottles.
Dad puts the pedal to the metal sends an arc of dirt and gravel
tires squealing as he pulls onto blazing blacktop.
Wind whips through open windows.
Mom's hair in waving tentacles all over the car.

She grabs the windowframe with one hand
bracing against Dad's speed
using her other hand to grab handfuls of hair
and gather it at her neck.
Ouch, you're on my hair.
She says this so often I don't even hear her.
I lean forward on the front seat
place my head between them
same as when I jump into their bed between body mountains
And ouch I'm on her hair again.

They sleep all day, sleeping off late nights and hangovers.
My energy bursting and missing theirs
I nestle in to soak up their mom and dad nests.
Today finally we are rushing towards cool water and
kids to play with.

Creamsicle juice runs down my arms,
dirt turning the drip lines brown
as I suck the stained wood stick.

We turn onto a dirt road
a wall of dust flies behind our Batmobile.
Gravel hits the car's underside in little pings and knocks.
The radio is static but he never turns it off.
He pops open a sweating green bottle of beer using his belt buckle,
takes a swig and passes it to Mom who drinks and returns it
to its holding place between his legs.

Our car is full of smoke, lighter fluid,
and the musty sex smell of worn Levis.
I know this smell from when I hug my parents around their legs
while they grind into each other and kiss.
I try to wedge my body in between them but they push me away.
This was us when we were together.

Dad pulls to the side of the dusty road downing milkweed
and I scramble to get out clutching a worn towel,
no need for bathing suits, we skinny-dip.

To get to the naked swimming hole
we climb under barbed wire fence.
The bank is steep and I grab handfuls of weeds
 tearing off the leaves,
feet stomping to find purchase, picking up speed,
and laughing at my own herky-jerky motion.

We pick our way through trees and branches to open riverbed.
rock molded by glacier, like the surface of the moon,
water thunders down in falls, collecting in clear cold pools.
Naked bodies everywhere, breasts and balls swinging.
children run screeching in the shallows.
longhaired men jump from the highest banks,
into deep pools, shooting up out of the water with joyous howls.

Women pass grainy snacks in bulk food bags
from health food store bins,
granola, dried fruit, chewy substances followed by cold beer.
I find friends and play horsy cantering into the water
kicking up spray with my hooves.
We build imaginary forts among the rocks with sticks.
where we will survive hunting buffalo
and cooking them over imaginary fires.

Dad squats on the rocks his long arms thrown over his knees
absently holding a burning Camel,
he passes a joint and talks stories.
It takes Daddy forever to get undressed and in the water
if he ever does,
he blames the ice-cold Maine ocean of his childhood.

He is lean and fair, blonde hair front and back,
sweaty armpit hair on everyone.
The swim a welcome bath for stinky hippie bodies,
flowery shampoos are passed between women.
They suds and rinse, bring dripping heads out of the water
refreshed and sweet smelling.

Barn Razing

My first kiss Tommy Toflin
in the hay loft till dawn's light striped through cracks
and knot holes in wide boards.
Hay is not fun to roll in, it scratches flesh red-raw
leaves your skin burning long after.
Tommy was a terrible kisser, drooled down my chin
his fingers gynecological in their probing.

The barn made me nervous
with my fear of spiders   speckled grey sacks
and the ladder to get up there
three stories straight up gave me vertigo.
Swinging my leg over the edge
to step onto the loft caused hours of anxiety.

Within its tall, tall sliding doors
a rusty tractor and combine,
sheep coming in and out chewing stupidly
I learned to milk goats here, get grain from the chute,
cut open fresh bales, stored my furniture between coastal moves.

Till it burned to the ground
the volunteer fire department hose
too late and too small for the blaze.
After it was gone leaving only a smoldered black square
Mom found pictures of the barn raising
Longhaired t-shirted hippies holding beer bottles and hammers
building the dream.

Mountain House

We slept on the lawn my first camping trip
aunts, uncles, and friends saw UFOs
from sleeping bags lined with red flannel
my cousin next to me on the lawn of the new house,
the empty house.
A grey shell of failing shingles, no floors, doors, just rafters.
A farmhouse from a bygone time in black and white photos
at town hall you could see the many farms, hotels,
even a bowling alley a hundred years before,
now cellar holes of lichen rock and tiger lilies
ghosts wearing the kind of bathing suits that come down the thighs,
the kind of farming that relied on horse and oxen.

A life much more glamorous in high white necks than ours
in the turn of the '70s to the '80s when everything went wrong.
When everyone you ever knew divorced.
Kramer vs. Kramer was the movie.
All the farming and windmills, long hair and alternative schooling
fumbled into single parent families and food stamps
this no man's land where us kids did not belong with the locals
and the hippies had all morphed into
new couples with new appliances.

This house with no floors was my home,
where I pinned pictures of Matt Dillon and Debbie Harry
a small blue Panasonic cassette player
brought Michael Jackson to the wilderness,
a kid who'd never heard Jackson 5
buying every Tiger Beat magazine
that could be found in the General Store.
Dad bought grinders and Coke for dinner,
AC/DC would replace my K-Tel tapes
and drywall would eventually fill in the gaps between two by fours.

TV was a black and white *Dukes of Hazzard,*
Dallas, and *General Hospital.*
Saturdays meant *Love Boat, Fantasy Island*
and some scary ass movies came on if you could stay awake.
But I was usually asleep on Dad's bed
right after Mr. Roarke said, "Welcome to Fantasy Island."

Dad stupidly loved this new blue world as much as me
we were strung out dragging those heavy ass batteries
to the neighbor's woodshed charger.
I wrote to my idol Blondie on puppy dog stationery,
waited for her limo to bottom out
on our washboard mountain road.

Dear John

We smoked puzzle grass,
wrote with twigs on white mushrooms.
Left the scars of our names on nature
as nature left on us, scrapes and puncture wounds,
a piece of us in the woods forever.

No amount of concrete or television
can erase the feeling of trees
sun filtering through leaves.
Our parents junk their cars
between Sugar Maples and White Pines
the old blue Chevy has been buried and so will we
be burnt to ash or laid down in a plain pine box.
Soft flannel and sawdust's clean smell —
that's what the filtered light is like.

Whip of milkweed sticky on red skin.
We steamed the flowers soft with butter.
Brown monarchs on Queen Anne's Lace
Black-eyed Susan in the hay fields —
the hay we will bale and lift with all our might
onto a wooden trailer behind a bright green tractor
John Deere.

99 Luft Balloons

As a child I was given a balloon
at Fayva shoe store with Mom.
I accidentally let go by the car's back door —
it flew from my hand, went up and up
fast with my screams.

High enough to see all of West Lebanon, New Hampshire —
how small and flat that mall surrounded by green,
how excruciating my disappointment.
I can still feel the distance between us.

I see everyone I care about as that balloon
rising up while I stand in a shitty parking lot
rubber boots, open mouth, tears streaming.

I steel myself against that moment,
save extra balloons in the pantry,
soak in aloneness on the edge of my bed,
ready myself for it.

I carry a big fat pin
to puncture red balloons
before they break my heart.

Fringe Elements

I was born to a second-generation atheist mother.
My father as much in love with every spiritual belief system,
mysticism, and religion as an agnostic Tibetan Buddhist can be.
There were no rules to be broken
but Dad did like the universe to revolve around his chair
and his storytelling.

Mom practiced some sort of spacey hippie practicality —
women were empowered by hard work: work-horse housework
gardening, baking, canning, drying, freezing.
The men took their sweet time
told their stories smoked ten joints
rolled endless tobacco, emptied six-packs
and eventually got around to fixing the cars
(more disassembling than assembling)
tilling the soil to plant Mom's seeds
they chiseled beams, built barns, and woodsheds.

Come fall we butchered pigs.
The men gathered round, stamping cold feet,
blowing clouds of breath, pickup trucks in a circle,
the dead pig chained to a tree, a bullet between the eyes
a knife to the throat, upside down, her pink body unzipped,
her guts removed and laid out on newspaper.
The women handled that stuff, filled pots with stinking innards.
Us kids we weren't horrified, we loved those pigs
but we knew the salty slices of bacon that would drape our plates,
the sausage, ham, the pork chops
with sage and thyme from Mom's garden.
We were pig meat too, we knew our meat was sweet pre-pubescent.
We understood fine lines and that sometimes they got crossed.
We were used to slaughter and the onslaught of men's eyes, hands.
We ran naked and barefoot with fat peaches under swelled bellies.

We took baths only when forced
left the tub ringed with garden dirt and duck pond mud.
We ate peanut butter with the oil on top
nuts poured into a grinder at the co-op
our food required a lot of chewing, a lot of cooking.
Mom had a pressure cooker that exploded now and then.

My memories of that time are small and dark as the dingy house
a white clapboard, the wood floor so rotten
there were pieces of plywood to cover the soft spots.
You had to know how to maneuver and I did,
I maneuvered myself into my favorite chair,
the seat of it caved caning
replaced by white clothesline wound around the frame.

The living room full of junk except a wall of records
a world of music I lived in: rock and roll, folk, and bluegrass.
And Mom's sewing table where she spread fabric, patterns,
and the leather she would paint designs on and cut into fringe
thousands of rustling leather strips decorating
every hippie's giggling body
and the creepy reach of acid's burning come down.
She made dolls for me there, heads of hair
made from long strips of leather
their bodies, like the ones I lived with,
had big bushes and bare breasts.

In the pit of the garage a cold cement hole smelled of motor oil
newts got trapped there sometimes
bright orange slivers, delicate dots decorating their backs
three fingers fine as purple thistle and dirty blonde hair.
After feeling their tiny feet run across mine
an apricot whisper fast then slow
I'd set them free, tangerine tail waving goodbye.

One day I'll wiggle into the woods
disappear under a bed of pine
rot into soil dark with life.

Wishing Well

We grew up with well water
problem was   and there was always a problem
come fall the spring dried up.
From our tap the last drops sucked through muck
dead red leaves   frogs sinking down into mud
hunkering in for the winter.
If only we could hibernate
shut down our needs before the frost blanket fell.

Winter mornings we threw buckets of yellow
from the back door into snow
bore hot holes to the brown grass below.
50-gallon drums filled from streams heated on the woodstove
that's how we washed ourselves in the years of *Dynasty*.
It's hard to feather your hair
with no electricity, Dad.

We had an empty room with hardwood floors
new wood window casings against white walls.
We imagined a toilet here and a bathtub
close to the furnace's iron grate.
I'd step out of the clawfoot tub onto a clean towel
a thousand times,
reach back to flush an imaginary chrome handle.

Everyday I passed that room on my way to the outhouse
and, Dad, you died a dreamer:
a Park Avenue kid with only a pot to piss in.

Runaway Collector

Dad always brought someone or something home
a fast driver with an eye for things on the side of the road
like the Stetson I had him cremated in.
He wore that hat for thirty-something years.
We found it on the side of the freeway brand new brown felt.

His mistake was those he chose to save, like John Blaze,
the horse who broke the fence and ran miles down the road
he ate all the bird seed from Dot Leisure's feeder.
She called the Game Warden and the State Police
her polyester mouth glued to the phone.
Her house aqua blue against pastoral green
the tacky Santa and reindeer never put away before Easter.
Took hours fading into the dark dots of dusk
for Dad to lasso that wild ass horse and ride him home.

One of his strays was a small brown duck
the other ducks gang-raped and pecked.
He scooped painted pond turtles
before they were flattened into dirt road.
Bear the dog ran at least sixty miles over hills and streams
back to the family we got him from.

My mom left soon after we moved in
stayed long enough to clear a road up there.
Cut a view across state to blue mountains seen from the kitchen
where she cooked breakfast on the woodstove.
Left the remnants of scrambled eggs on the ceiling
was gone before the first snow fell.

The girlfriend he married, divorced,
and carried on with for twenty years, a rescue.
He picked her out of a tarpaper shack

with two dirty-nosed kids and multiple personalities
though I never saw even one.

Life on that hill left all of us ready to run.

Busy Town

I remember what dead hands feel like
and they're not worth holding.

I remember when I asked you to smash my Fisher Price
push-popper so I could get the gumballs out
even though I knew they weren't really gumballs.
You smashed it with your sledgehammer.

I liked to steal your Smith Bros coughdrops
black licorice and Luden's lemon from the glove box,
how your jaw clicked when you bit into an Almond Joy
or a Pecan Pie from the village store,
how we didn't tell Mom about the sweets.

I remember when Franny Bear came home leaking red pools,
you examining her furry body and exclaiming
a bullet had gone clean through.
All those other dogs you straddled on the kitchen floor,
pulled quills from whining snouts with needlenose pliers.

The stories you read *Wind in the Willows*,
Frog and Toad, and Richard Scarry —
Personified animals hold you the most.

You liked to get stoned and watch people
in their little cars and trucks buzz around New England towns
imagine them as Richard Scarry characters
Lowly Worm in his apple car,
the Beagle policeman.
You'd laugh with such abandon.
I remember.

Maybe It *Is* a Love Story
(for Angel)

She did love him, had dreams of him since childhood
her dream reoccurring like their affair.

In her dream he was tall blonder than sugar crystals
eyes so blue and wild they'd make you squint
his lips beyond vitruvian proportion
those of an African prince on a white man.

They met a party at his pad
she was eighteen tagging along with her older brother
Her name Georgina, Dinny for short
her legs anything but and on they went tan and elegant
brunette bob and a sparkle in her eye.

He was an inferno, his blonde like white fire
a ponytailed hipster, his carpenter jeans stained to a fine finish.
He spun tales of riding Little Joe under western stars
to the velvety underground of New York City's bars

John Dallett he was beat.
He wrapped the rap of the Buddhists at the Bick.
Turned the youngsters on with the I Ching,
and ran a communication network for the scene
from a bulging black leather address book.

He loved books,
spoke of Celine, Unamuno, and *The Monk*,
and he loved women.
When the party ended, he knelt by her chair
whispered in her ear to stay and she did.

She knew him as the man in her dream
knew he was significant but not why

so that night she did stay, lay in all those words
all that philosophizing, storytelling and lovemaking.
And left pregnant with all the blonde light of him
all the flame of nervous energy and spirit wound too tight
mixed with all the leggy colt of her.

He saw the baby girl once, after a show at the Club 47
He met the grandparents, rode horses,
looked into tiny blue eyes, his own corn silk hair.
Went back to Harvard Square, made sandals, smoked dope
got carted off to the nuthouse, then moved to Vermont.

She married a lawyer, safer bet
they moved to Africa to save the world.
Later, they landed across the river from John
raised families as strangers, sisters and brothers unknown.

After divorces and well into their forties, they tried it again.
He drove to her lofts and touchy feely parties.
She made him a little sweeter, a taste softer
than he'd been as a married man but he was still flaky,
smoked too much pot and she had to move on.

Before he died, they did it once more
his blood pressure medicine thwarting her best efforts
his mind consumed with his lame girlfriend
and the endless caretaking she needed from him
she was broken so he was never out of a job.
And Dinny didn't need a thing, she really never had.

She loved him, still saw him as the young man in the dream.
The knowledge seeker, wrestler of truth and substance
lover of complex science and cornball TV.
In the ridiculous he found beauty, hoarded it in small metal boxes.
But he was too stagnant, stuck in a rut
spinning his wheels only to marvel at the mud's flight.

When he died, she was there
the ex-wives came to the memorial,
but she was there at his bedside.
She knew another him a dreamy man,
light blinding as an angel's feather.

Knotty Heart

We explore junk piles and you admire tree stumps
they remind me of home like chainsaws.
I want to take you there through trees holding hands.
But I don't know where home is.
Mom and Geoff's is not mine
a cabin in the woods full to the roof with them,
not any of me, save for the school photos of my son that I've sent.

I have no history there.
The houses I grew up in, Dad's houses,
are standing but have been gutted to the studs.
Remodeled minus the nicotine yellowed walls,
chewed up floorboards,
full of droppings and animal fur.
These gamey places I grew up in are as distant
as a place can be in the same lifetime.

I'm a time traveler trying to explain to you how we lived.
How good a carrot tastes with the dirt still on,
how hardened your soles become barefoot all summer long,
dodging perverts and drunks at your own kitchen table
under layers of smoke in the dragon's lair.

No one drives those old cars anymore,
kids rattling around the backseat
loose and unstrapped,
wild as bobcats with pointy ears
listening, waiting, to lead me back through time.

Feeding the Mountain

I cremated the smoker
a craving to the bone turned to ash.
My daddy sprinkled in the snow
bone fragments in white cold
barren stalks on a colorless day.
I hate winter.

Sorry, Daddy, that's when people die
even your summer solstice self
better seen in pocketed t-shirts
blue like your eyes lighting fires, driving fast
with the windows down to the stock car races
or the drive-in.

That carnivorous winter comes around fast
that walk up the mountain and to the out-house.
You snow plowing and wood splitting
woolen pants held with suspenders
Pac boots over wool socks with the red tops.

You dressed like those old country men
but your suspenders had rainbows
and you said, "Nanoo nanoo," a Cheshire grin on your face.
You had stories for days but you wore them out
talked that same old shit no one wanted to hear
those last years till you died
and we missed you.

Things I Learned from Mom

How to make some kick-ass scrambled eggs when I was six
to use no ingredients with label or instruction
unless they came from the *Joy of Cooking*.

She told me kissing was okay but not to fuck
on my way to sleep out with a group of boys in a hunting trailer
me in a sleeping bag between two guys
their fingers inside me all night
the grey light tree shadows, crickets roaring at us,
about the end of childhood and
the walk back to the house in the morning
when I peed my Levis from holding it in.

My mother taught me about work
fingers bulging with veins from days in cold
hammering nails, lifting 2x4s, stirring cement powder,
and digging, digging, dynamiting.
Knowing how to build something out of nothing.

Picking berries and walking slowly to the house
she hums while making a pie or a cheesecake from scratch.
She sings bluegrass songs the way I sing Keith Sweat & Mary J.
Her whole heart telling the stories of disappointment,
of marriages left in moments of self preservation,
dummying up, laying on her back
whooping up those fake orgasms.

Her thumb sideways in her mouth and looking down
while they talk in big voices over her
needy boys, these men she married.

She works steadfast till her back hunched forward
like the grandmas in Chinatown.

Her hair, the same hippie-chick style since age fourteen,
has fallen out from a drug cocktail
the trial to save her liver almost killed her.
Dehydrated and shivering under heated blankets, she wouldn't quit.
That's what she taught me — perseverance:
tight lipped, bent into the wind, she goes on.

Care Giving

I tell my mother I want to break up with Mike.
She says she can't imagine being alone
and what would she have done these last few weeks she's been sick
if her man hadn't fed her, shampooed her hair,
rubbed on her cream, and brought the jugs of water
she was required to drink.

I stammer and somehow never get out
that I would move out there, I would take care of her.
That's what people do, of course.
I'm too caught up thinking how Mike likes to take care of me
when I'm sick or tired. How he comes to my bedside
every day with coffee and ice water. Massages my aches
and gets no pussy or praise in return.
I can get old with this.

But right now I'm not old. Right now
I'm supposed to be living. The big faces on the tabloids
are women my age in evening gowns and bikinis
on second or third marriages traveling with hot young guys.

If I tell my mom I'm sick of sleeping with him,
want somebody else, she'll think I'm crazy.
If I tell her I want to break up with him because
he's broke and I'm tired of supporting him and his kids
she'll understand.

She might even tell me I have to end it immediately
like the psychiatrist did, sent me out sobbing, never to return.
You're co-dependent the shrink said. That word
defining love and everything I've ever known about it.

I personally believe that marriage could not exist
without at least one co-dependent.
My mother would laugh at that label, as she does all
labels and twelve steps and other New Agey bull crap.
(Actually the phrase New Age would be too new age for her.)

When she did go to couples counseling
somewhere after twenty-five years together
she said it made everything worse, that instead of the big issues
like his kids not talking to him, the devastations of
irresponsible parenting, he pulled out stuff like
She never leaves the butter dish out.
I always have to get it from the fridge.
It's too hard and it rips my toast.

In Dreams

I ride Muni buses up winding unpaved dirt roads
to kitchens where brothers blast beat boxes on Duracell D's
there ain't no outlets in this kerosene lit,
woodstove warmed, car part cluttered, once abandoned farmhouse.
We watch *General Hospital* on black and white 12-inch screen
run off a 12-volt battery lugged in from the car.

In my dreams I still feel Nike tread on my face
Whispers of *I love you* and *bitch I'll kill you* in ex's embrace
I wake in a sweat when my skinhead
and basketball bouncing boyfriends cross time
and come face to face.

A tangled child alone and bored at home
I dug crates of dusty books and scratched albums
remnants of city lives before my parents' move
that pushed us deeper into the woods to the homegrown
vegetables, grass, hops from fertile earth fed in autumn
flaming red and orange leaves. We try to dress louder
so hunters won't mistake and shoot us between our doe like eyes.

Cow shit smelling Future Farmers of America
taunt me from the front of the yellow school bus
about my bald head, burnt crucifix, combat boot sneer.
The brothers sing "The Freaks Come Out At Night"
on the 22 back to Fillmore laugh at how unfuckable I am.
Months later they are asking for my number
my hair grown out, rocking new Reeboks in time to PE and Eric B.

I trudge barefoot to outhouses
down railroad flat halls to water closets
both too claustrophobic for closed doors.
My pissy ghetto elevators let me out on mountain tops

where snow piles and hardens till it cuts my thighs
as I step in sinking down and down to the frozen ground.

I speed country roads, Daddy behind the wheel
maneuvering deer crossings and head-on collision
he talks his blue streak but I never hear.

The outsider I still am awake
keeps shedding skins, a shy smiling snake.

I Am That House

we bought when I was ten
the rotten one   no floors to speak of
snakes in the clapboard   raccoon scat
and remnants of squatting Hari Krishnas
disciples of the blue-bodied boy.

We were not the first hippies to touch down
on that moon soil —
we changed everything
but the overall decay.

Dad found comfort in the decrepit
left me always trying to put things in their place
these days I don't trust my own decisions
I'm running out of stories
ready to fall back in love, he pulls away
I'm confused enough to follow.

These woods are dark
with I told you so.

I Was the Girl They Whispered About

Big as I was I still felt the brush of balled paper and orange peels
bounce off my shoulders on the school bus.
Me stubbornly staring out the window in my Dad's Chevy cap.
When I finally got up the nerve to look back
everything went blurry, a swirl of pale faces
like the girls in the *Carrie* locker room
and I'd wonder if I was just paranoid.

By high school being whispered about was a challenge
each day I'd confront them more outrageous
hair chopped ragged with sewing scissors
dresses made from pillowcases
armholes cut near the top of my Sponge Bob shoulders
the bottom just shy of my crotch, thick thighs pushing it up
daring them in their Izods, Levis, and shit-kickers
to look, to say anything —
they'd whisper, snicker, seemed to already know
who I'd fucked at the party on Friday.
Only the art teachers loved me:
I made earrings from Barbie accessories
collaged crazy things and liked spraypaint.
Other teachers grew nervous, I was too serious, too fidgety,
a scribble of writing on a wrinkled paper, a C- at best.

On Haight Street they still whispered,
the girlfriends hated me, I only hung around dudes,
was more comfortable around testosterone and violence.
A drunk kid, I got my combat boots twisted behind my ears
by young punks in alleys. Afterwards they laughed and whispered
but none of them wanted to fight me.

The City Out of Order

In The City once a year it's hot enough to ride the 5 Fulton
to Ocean Beach where crashing surf eats sand by the mile.
An undertow so hungry it pulls icy toes out from under you,
you can only get more than a foot in
if you are drunk, drunk, drunk, malt liquor Mickey's
40-ounce drunk and I got in to my shoulders that way once.
A sensation colder than my whole snowy upbringing.

We were teenagers skipping down Haight Street
Suzy in the lead, always climbing to the top of light poles,
teetering on the edges of cliffs.
She was carrying a mylar balloon that night,
lost it around Clayton in front of the fruit stand
it flew right up into Muni lines sparks rained down
and store windows fell into darkness
roaring and cheering, we ruled the city.

All those times we had to fix the glass front door,
all those bodies launched through it drunk and desperate to feel.
Slamming the gate, shaking the flat, calling down to Johnson's
and scraping up the money to replace the glass again.
Suzy kicking and screaming that she wasn't scared,
she would fight us all.

Once we were partying in a flat down on San Jose Ave
we had to pull Danny Lucky off her
his teeth sunk deep in her forehead.
Once I left them in my room while we went up to Rampage Radio
we returned deep in Jack Daniels and found
every poster lopsided all the furniture upside down.
Danny and Suzy more into killing each other than fucking.

My City was Bags the Skinhead,
I shaved my head traded squeaky combat boots
for Doc Marten's and braces,
circled the block all day long to be near him.
On my knees, bent over at parties, blacked out in alleys,
trying to get closer.

When we were alone we talked and fucked all night,
did speed in the pink palace, spent the night at my aunt's.
Alone at night I crossed my fingers
asked God to make him love me, make me his woman.
Tall, muscled, tatted, an ex-hippie when drunk enough
he played his flute and I followed.

I walked home alone, beer cans hurled from cars through Fillmore
I took dangerous routes on purpose because the city was mine.
Three a.m. a guy walked out of the Palladium
punched me dead in the face and just kept walking,
he probably thought I was a dude standing there with a bald head
in my drunk haze, on the way to the pit to drink more beer.

In San Francisco I sat in the bleachers at Hamilton Recreation
watching my boyfriend Dre play basketball.
My hair grown out, still wearing fishnets from the old days
but sucking candy sticks and trying to act all cute and sassy
like the black girls. I was his girl and we rode the bus on dates
in my letterman jacket and Reeboks.

We drank milkshakes and rocked Stan Smiths. He claimed me.
We beat the shit out of each other. His feet and fists crushing me,
his flesh under my nails, breaking me, holding keys
scarring his face, him chasing me, me chasing him,
me filling sunglasses with tears and black eyes.
Him spending his first night in jail after they led him out,
the cops finding me in the closet, a pile of purple bruise.

My first night in jail Cookie was one of my cellies,
brown scars covered her limbs.

She was Greek had a lived a life more than heroin but you couldn't
tell by looking at her. I was a kid who'd never changed in a locker
room, never dressed for gym, flunked in fact, but stood in dirty
water, naked like everyone else.

They called me Brooke Shields.
Hey, Brooke, what you in here for, a B case?
Prostitution was always assumed, I was white and not strung out.
What else could it be?

Truth is jail freed me,
from me
so alone.

Pacifica x 3

I.
I ended up there when I was fifteen
riding between two Skinheads from LA in a small pickup truck.
Don't know where they picked me up from
but we roared around Civic Center in the dark
pushing each other in an abandoned wheelchair by the fountains
where people pissed and drank beer in the urine spray.

They mugged a suit by City Hall
knocked him down and took his wallet.
I jumped on his back at a full run heard a dull grunt
We were frying, high, felt all *Clockwork Orange* and shit.
Violence on acid such a disappointing concept.

They took me to a girl's house in the nightmare suburbs.
Her fireplace made of big ugly fake rock.
The houses pink and blue lined up like baby teeth along the hills.
I was frightened, had to spend the whole night stranded
while the idiot girl showed us her mother's plus size lingerie
and the high wore off into dirty.

II.
Once I went there to see the ocean.
The waves were huge on the rocks, spectacular.
We rode with some people my aunt's boyfriend sold weed to.
Stuck in the back of the tin can van
with a guy in a wheelchair pissing into a milk jug.
Fuck the ocean, I wanted to get back to the Haight.

III.
The third with a Cholo riding low in a '64 Impala.
Winnie met him at 850 Bryant
picked me and Judy up we made him cruise the whole city.

We ended up at his mom's place in Pacifica
He invited us into the bathroom where I sat on the closed toilet
Winnie perched on the edge of the bathtub.
He offered us heroin.
I said yes, she said ok.
It was her he wanted to screw and her he fixed first.
I don't think he gave me a thing in my shot.
Then he did himself, nodding into the mirror
a bloody needle hanging from his neck.

Judy called us from the front
the guy's mom was home not real happy
about the young Chinese girl in her living room.

He drove us back to Haight Street
Winnie threw up on the sidewalk
and our whole world
changed.

Girl Cuffed

Cuffed red spraypaint hands
extra large drunk girl
hiding behind extra small bush
even my friends laughed at me
picked up from Park Street Station
shame faced, hanging-over.

Cuffed to the dumpster
In the back of Cala Foods
drunk again, I threw a ham in my flight jacket.

Cuffed to fifteen underage hands
A human chain snaking out and down cold ass on concrete
in the parking lot next to the On Broadway
In the paddy wagon they rifled through my girlfriend's bag
of stolen lingerie and Seagram Seven —
lucky girl, she'd been in the bathroom
when the fire marshal and the cops came backstage.

Cuffed downtown
security followed us from Macy's to Market Street.
They threatened us with grand theft
called us malicious and posted our cute bad-girl Polaroids.

Cuffed on a Market Street island
I fought Ross's security and a traffic cop
dropping my swollen bags of loot
they called it assault and theft.
I was no longer a minor.

Cuffed in a paddy wagon
from North Station to 850
watching a junkie kick the doors

till actually   miraculously
the door bent and he slipped out wafer thin
onto littered Tenderloin streets to his next fix.

Cuffed face down
cheek on the yellow line, shotguns at my head
Cadillac Seville smoking behind me.

Cuffed in Fillmore
perp walked past my ex's rear window
bullet casings everywhere
all the neighbors said it was the big white girl.

Cuffed behind my '66 Impala
pukey juniper citrus smell of spilled gin and juice
walked heel to toe, counted fingers backwards
until a second car pulled up flashing
GI Joe with a Breathalyzer.

Cuffed at the bottom of the stairs
when the beer soaked cop loosened his headlock
on my kicking body I hit the stairs running
straight into the waiting squad car
police radios blaring catch the girl in green.

Cuffed on a frigid night in reverse
avoiding a roadblock on the beltway
stripped of license and car   cursing frozen clouds
rip-throwing the pile of tickets all that cold walk home.

Cuffed in my living room
smart-ass cop trying to hustle me out in my socks
still Public Enemy #1
over a noise warrant.

Hot Pants
(for Stephie)

She was an honors student who dropped acid,
sold weed and did her homework by street light
while her boyfriend carried stereos and TVs from people's homes.

Her first job was at Mr. Donut where
Mr. Seaburger leered at her and the other young girls
through his coke bottle glasses.
Mr. Grabass Seaburger paid one dollar ten cents
plus tips, and that was after a raise.
Still she felt guilty for pocketing three or four bucks a night.

Her friends would pick her up after work in a custom van
the next day she'd show up hung-over
drop cans of Bavarian cream scooping it by the handful
off the dirty floor to fill the donuts.

Right before her eighteenth birthday
she went on a real job hunt.
In hot pants and stilettos, hair feathered fiercer than Farrah Fawcett
she walked into the ABC Liquor store and bar.

A biker hang-out, it was not unusual for a Harley
to be parked right on the throbbing disco floor.
The manager told her he was interested
but first she'd have to take a lie detector test,
Sure she would flunk and with no idea what they would ask,
she let them hook her up to the machine.

They asked if she'd ever smoked marijuana
then continued through a long list of drugs
No she said, hands shaking.
She'd taken them all since the age of ten
starting with a summer in Vermont at her sister's house.

She thought it was over when
they asked if she'd stolen from a job.
No, never she said again.
Clearly they could see she was lying.

But a few days later
the manager called and offered her the job.
Since applying she had turned eighteen.
When she showed them her new ID
and they realized they had hired her with a fake
they thought it was hilarious.

One day while stocking shelves
she went to the back for more booze.
She ran right into the store manager, the general manager,
and the bouncer.
The little group looked up at her with glassy eyes
arms tied off as they passed around a syringe of heroin.

Suddenly it all made sense —
the lie detector and all the crazy questions
were a test, a test to see how down she was.
She had passed the test proved she was down,
down to the ground.

School Daze

I never succeeded at much
but I made it here and want to celebrate
It's boring, I admit, my classmates' asses
are no doubt sweaty and numb like mine
from hard plastic and middle school stage lights.

Our high school so small we had to borrow an auditorium
for our little graduation.
On stage we glow in red robes
with outfits underneath painstakingly picked out
we come from families that don't graduate much.

My black dress was boosted,
pushed deep into a trench coat pocket
can't believe I'm graduating,
I just kept showing up at the school house,
just had nothing better to do, got more action with the brothers
a few onstage with me now I fucked
and shared forties with, sold stolen dime sacks to.

My parents are three thousand miles away
but I have family in the audience.
My auntie and her boyfriend, a couple of my drop-out friends,
from the stage I can see them ducking in and out of their seats
to do lines of speed in the bathroom.
Later they'll complain about how long and boring
the ceremony was and I'll ignore them and their drugs.

I'll drink mine, rot gut Cisco
get rip torn enough to stop wondering
what the hell I'm going to do next.

Ocean Beach Babylon
(for Brad, 5/9/1970 - 4/23/2012)

When I stopped doing drugs my friends were just getting started.
Fighting in their underwear over needles
and dope in the light of our front door.
From the top of the stairs I scream at them to shut the fuck up.
I worked all night on phone sex lines and I'm just trying to sleep.

Brad screams back at me calls me a bitch,
says it's no wonder that my boyfriend beat the shit out of me.
A nigger that's what he calls me.
His face is a mask of dope and sickness.
I'm already down my boyfriend just stomped me into the ground
while saying he loved me.
I don't speak to Brad for years.

He goes to jail then prison, violates parole every eighteen months,
and spends close to a decade behind bars.
I forgive and live, but I never forget.
That early morning scuffle on the stairs
how quickly he turned on me.
Me, trying to keep it all together, rent paid and the phone on.

Brad was once my best friend, he was even a boyfriend.
Stood on his tiptoes the first time we kissed
at a party, his girlfriend scared of me, the big skinhead girl.
We were thrown down two flights of stairs
by the bouncers for drinking straight from the keg
and stealing the donations.

We left his girlfriend at the party and got stung by bees
hiding from the cops in Golden Gate Park.
Fucked on the roof of Chinese Projects
staring drunkenly over the twelve story edge,

defying gravity and the cold we tried to sleep up there
made it home on the bus where he lived with me
till he went back to Juvenile Hall.

When he escaped he went with my best friend
but it was cool he was one of us
and he went out with all of us over the years.
At parties me or him always got in a fight
swinging through the crowd to the other's side.
We were 86ed from everywhere.
We shared blonde hair, high cheekbones,
and something that ate at us from the inside out.

Six years after the stairs Brad called me up.
Said he'd heard I wanted to talk but couldn't believe it.
He was an ex-con tattooed Dirty White Boy across his back.
From segregation back to our yellow crew
of half black and Chinese babies.
I always dated black guys had even left him for one.
I never knew where that left us,
except friends, cause he had to do what he had to do
on the inside and I understood that, sort of.

We got together went out to the beach.
sat on the wall drinking and telling stories
History ate at us like the waves ate the sand.
At nightfall bonfires lit the beach
we were sure we'd find the heads and parties of our past.

Instead the clumps of bodies we eased into were dry
fire warmed faces grilling hot dogs, popping sodas.
Church groups invited us to join.
Back in the day it would have been Sunset Pods,
Headbangers or Skins lighting up the beach
scattering from cops searchlights.

Our adventures had been stolen and replaced
with squeaky clean church folk.

It was tragic and scary or maybe we were.
Maybe they invited us to church
cause our asses needed to be saved.

Nothing to Hold You Down on Market Street

Between bus stops you realize you don't have a home
some days you walk the sparkly sidewalks blind with sadness
as useless as all the other trash blowing along
in the violent Pacific air
outdoor fuschia trees and aloe lose their magic
just overgrown houseplants
that have gone astray, like you.

The fog is not romantic. It enters your bones cold,
ends the lie that is California.
This is the city you needed, you jonesed for
and there's no home to go back to,
no quaint New England bed of
spindle and patchwork. This is it.

But nothing holds you here.
The mates you pick bob around the ring,
you try and you try to beat them into needing you
you punch them in the nose with your little girl fists
you kick and feed them your icky bits.

You want to force them to hold you
safe as mother arms in the night
again and again you wake alone
every day a hangover even
when you're too bored to drink
too tired to twelve step.

Some people have things they went to school for
things that pay them or require them: children, careers,
foreign words. You only wanted love
you'll only kill it when it's given
feels like putting on someone else's clothes.

You can't fit into it
are too malnourished to swallow it,
need something stronger
to keep you from falling off,
right off this quaky edge of continent.
All you can do is walk and walk,
let the Muni bus pass your broke ass by.

Leaving Court Ordered Therapy

I stared out the passenger window
at grey snowbanks walling in narrow streets.
Squeezed into the front seat next to Mom and Geoff.
I was trapped, in snow, in cold, in hated winter.
I was a bull crashing around a tiny town.

Mom asked how it went.
It took me a minute to get the words out,
It made me want to drink more, it's just depressing!
I said, my voice cracking.

Trying to convince a therapist you're not a drunk
may be the thing that makes you want a drink
more than you ever have.
When I filled out the intake questionnaire,
I had tried to make it sound like I was a social drinker,
who was only social now and again.
But I had blown a .38 blood alcohol content
and even with all the lying,
taking a sliver of truth off here and there.
The guy told me I needed counseling for sure.
I was a drunk at age 25.

It wasn't so much the alcohol I was addicted to
as the bootless men, or my fitful attachment to them.
It shifted from one to the other and left me
with no one to love but 40 ounces of Crazy Horse.
Seagram's Gin and grapefruit juice
probably my longest relationship.
I reeked of it when I got pulled over that dark night
leaving the club where I had been kicking the shit out of some
young girl who was hanging out with my younger boyfriend.
I had jumped in my car, smashed around corners

and almost hit a man in the crosswalk when they nabbed me.
A big cup of drink spilling in my driver's seat when I got out.
Still, I thought I might drive away from the flashing lights
until the second car came with the Breathalyzer.

My voice rising, I was yelling at Mom now,
Maybe I am a drunk 'cause I hate my life so much.
It does make me want to drink I wailed.
And Mom understood me when I yelled this
She said something like *I know*
It was one moment in the mess of my life
when I knew she got it.
She probably wanted a drink too.
I was no easy daughter to have.

Still it was pitiful, anyone else —
well, anyone who wasn't an alcoholic
(which I really believed I wasn't) —
would have committed themselves to the therapy, the court ordered
program, the school, the getting their life together trip back east
I was supposedly on.
Me, I kept tearing mine apart, getting further and further
from the responsible adult I should have been growing into.

After the arrest I had gone to court, then the program with
all the questionnaires. A guy with a big mustache looked bored by
the steady stream of under-the-influence desperadoes
pushing through his brown doors. He sent me here to one of the
therapists off his list. It was the second one I'd been to, and
I was just lying the whole time and the lying made me feel
I must really have something to hide, and feeling
like I had something to hide, made me feel like a piece of shit.
I had held it together in there. But when I got outside to
Mom's old rusty white Firebird in those old rusty snowbanks
and they asked me how it had gone, I broke down.

I didn't go back, I didn't get therapy, I didn't get my license back,
or my car, or my nursing license.

I just couldn't go back and pay money to a therapist
I couldn't actually talk to.

On Bush Street

My window looks into an airshaft
dark and musty with smells of foreign foods and aging hoarders.
Ten people sleep in the studio on the other side.
My other window looks at a wall
painted grey streaked white with shit.

The pigeons outside drive Moxie my cat to grow wings.
The studio smells of 409 and heat,
a muggy New York City summer
trapped inside San Francisco walls.
The hooker downstairs tells me the former tenant
died on the twin mattress where I sleep.
The southern white landlord asks me to leave
makes up lies about my black boyfriend and my black cat.

Moxie leaves me a gift in the middle of the apartment
placed on a pyramid of shredded paper towels —
a dead mouse.

850 Bryant

Went to jail today to get a rap sheet
through metal detectors and elevators out of a '60s police show
found the right room down a long marbled hall
of plexiglass windows
people shuttling in and out of doors with numbers on them.

Memories float up from downstairs
paneled courtrooms where this future was decided long ago
nerves balanced on folding wood chairs or worse
the holding cell out back cement seat, cement walls
toilet paper roll for pillow in a hard box of back pain
and hemorrhoids.

You wore orange sweats like every other antsy person
in this tight space, smells brown like wet paper towels.
Wait for your name, eat lunch from a small cardboard box,
dry bread a packet of mustard.

You waited and you waited no makeup or hairbrush,
only a small black comb raw porous skin under fluorescent light.
Ill fitting orange always looks guilty in front of the judge.
Un-cuffed for a minute the public pretender plays the role.
An over the shoulder look at the wooden chairs
but no one is there for you.

Back to the holding cell
through the maze of granite behind chambers
echoing with keys and deputy's black shoes.
A future doomed to return here some day
even if not in custody.

To go to a little window on one of these floors
between the cells upstairs and the courtrooms down

ask for printed numbers on a page
case numbers, violation numbers, docket numbers
numbers that represent who you were, what you did
and what you are allowed to become.

These numbers have followed you through life.
Many times you placed a thumb, rolled it,
gave up another, then all of them
slowly rolling, giving up your magnificence
an art display you were born with
your very own map
of future and past.

Drunk School 2011

I did graduate nursing school
with a cast on my arm, a fat lip, and a black eye.
I never got my nursing license but I made the grade,
passed the state exams but the DUI kept me from getting licensed.
I needed to prove I had taken care of things I hadn't.

The night before graduation
I saw my young boyfriend with a young girl.
He wasn't my boyfriend anymore
I had left him for his friend (who had gone back to his wife)
I was back sleeping with the young one again,
coming from a bar I saw him
went fucking crazy pushed him, kicked him,
threw his boom box in the street.

I ran up the hill to his apartment
He came in as I was hurling the coffee table against the wall,
threw me down the stairs. My wrist bone snapped neatly in two.
It was a hot, achy hangover and self inflicted heartbreak.

Fast forward, sixteen years —
I'm a mom, I have a job, own a home, pay taxes,
haven't been arrested in all those years.
I go to renew my California Driver's License
and they tell me there is a hold from the state of Vermont.

I spend the next year trying to clear it up —
spend fifteen-minute breaks on
phone calls and faxes to an office in Vermont.
It's only open one hour a week eastern time
and holds a woman mean as a viper.
(I assure her I did not kill her family member
or anyone else while driving under the influence.)

She says my name *C-a-s-s-a-n-d-r-a* real shitty
like maybe I'm slow.

After months of back and forth
I find out it's just one piece of paper they want —
just a standard printout from the DMV — to get into a DUI class.
I am classified as a Wet Reckless (story of my life)
which is the envy of the intake room.
I only have to go to six weeks of classes,
most have six months or a year,
and we are a mixed bag of bitter nuts
in this depressing East Oakland classroom.

I run into old schoolmates
and spend the next six (which turns to eight) weeks
watching films about tragic accidents and
recovering alcoholics. There are many class clowns.
The teacher is a heavy-set black woman with a long wavy braid
and a crazy sense of humor. Her teaching style is one of telling
stories
none of which have a damn thing to do with why we are here.
In fact the punishment of attending is
the only actual rehabilitative aspect to this thing.

People tell their stories but it's no AA meeting
everyone here came in a car driven on a suspended license
and everyone here is going to have a drink when they leave.
There are toothless dope fiends, young girls with bad weaves,
a cowboy in full hat, buckle, and boots.

We are Latino, Asian, Black, and White.
We ask stupid questions and laugh.
A white boy sits next to me scribbling things the teacher says
in his notebook, he thinks she's so funny.
She reminds me of an ex-boyfriend's sister
and I'm thinking I don't know where he's from
but this is your standard jailhouse, welfare to work,
work furlough, drug program classroom.

I've seen plenty: plastic chairs, stained carpet, fluorescent lights, and a fat lady with all the control at the front of the room.

Exposed

I was coming from San Quentin,
where I visited my boyfriend every weekend
spent my days being bodily searched
to sit in a visiting room and be interrogated.

He had nothing better to do than dream up ways to pick me apart.
My need to confess led me to expose myself
in a room of splintered families and correctional officers
monitoring stolen affection.

You can touch twice:
once when your prisoner comes in,
once when you say goodbye,
the clang of steel at our backs
the CO's command to squat and cough.

On the outside I passed a postcard perfect bay,
waited for, rode visitor vans to Muni buses.
It took hours to reach home's lonely walls.

On the 38 Geary I sit in the back
a car comes alongside
I double-take at dick in hand.
The driver is leering at me
jacking while driving in broad daylight.

Around me all the riders stare ahead
no one sees this.
I wanted to scream, laugh, point.
I look back and big dick speeds away,
proud of himself, it was funny.

Two days later coming from work in the Financial District
panty-hosed and conservative I board the number 7.
A normal-looking white man gets on a few stops later
and sits in the back seat across from me.
I'm drowsy and warm in the sun
when out of the corner of my eye I see flesh
bobbing up and down
I turn to see him grinning at me flicking his stiff dick
It bounces and smiles a purplish hello.

I turn back to the window in silence
I want to make fun of him, turn him into victim
but I do nothing
surrounded by passengers on a spring afternoon
my eyes are locked on Market Street
wondering if I had imagined
the naked gun at my back.

Slippery When Wet

The wind holds the words of a lover. He calls
from behind a trash can in a building of sick people.

In this wind storm the lover I belong to snores at my side.
Watering cans, pieces of lattice clatter across the back porch
with hot pink petals.

Inside me something else burns hot pink restless
but I stay, spill the ice water he brought
rub the eye cream around aging orbs.
Little lights hit the window create the rocking atmosphere
of a boat and we are adrift.

In a confusing world of want
the hunger isn't filled by green curry last night
or handmade tortillas this morning
only fattened.

Greedy and lazy it wants something
for nothing.
A lover on the side,
an income
without a job.

It's the Speed, Stupid

It's the speed that ruined your life,
not some girl named Julie.
It's the soul crunching depression of Meth.
The shit that leaves your skin cracked open
your insides too parched to bleed out.

Bone rubbing bone
you wore out your gristle.
You jerked that thing raw.
Sat on the curb crying into your doll lashes.
Other men had to turn away.
Still you blame us cold fish women.

You stick your tongue in empty baggies search for residue.
Something that once felt good leaves you
with only a sleeping bag in a cold alley.
It's seduction stronger than mine
my pampered foot in your mouth.

Can't you see
no one wants eyes like that,
they belong on velvet paintings,
on third world faces
empty bowls for flies to drink.
We need shades to look into the burn.

But you don't call it high
unless it's mainlined
even, if your mouth is so dry
I can hear the sound a room away
membrane minus the mucous
leather-mouth jacket.

That look is a sign on your back
Kick Me Please
I understand if I'm the bad guy
speed can be the good cop
and I refuse to put that fat suit on.

Nebulous or Not

My secrets are young black men
Yours, small white rocks
Mine text late on Friday nights
Yours call in a throaty whisper
From SROs in the Tenderloin
As much home as not having a home
It's been part of you all along
We are runaways
You too tall Spanish speaker
Too long gone with long-legged blondes.

You know all my bad stories
felt the pounding of sneaker tread
from my ex kicking us both in the head
first time drunk in my bed
since then you understand my dangerousness
the thugs I'm tethered to
and I saw you those years all spun out
rocketing down cable car hills
drum solos in the air
eyes big enough to fall in
I stepped back on the curb
my old friend red-faced and ashy
the way speed freaks get.

I hate when your eyes have no edges
mouth crackles deserted
brain zooming logic checked out
the unwinnable race
rabbit down the hole trick
dope fiends always think they can win.
Sober, you're my best friend
and I don't tire of being compared

to the first five minutes of *Star Wars*.
I kind of like being your world.

To the Courier of Love
(A bike messenger on Valentine's Day)

Today I want to ride on your handlebars
climb into your messenger bag
hug your skull like your beanie hat.
Wish you'd whisper into me
the radio clipped close to your mouth
above your scarred collarbone.
After work I'll slide into you
with the beers and the whiskey
hot in your gut.

Yesterday I turned away your eager cold air kiss
hated the flush of your cheeks reddened at the bar
neglected your legs and your arms
tired from peddling hills and alleys
pushing your bike on and off the train
up and down the stairs, chain ticking
as you coast the streets home.

I can't promise I'll be better despite my wanting to.
I'm here, uncombed in my old bathrobe and fuzzy slippers
looking like a crazy housewife and I am crazy
but I can't be your wife 'cause I can't love you back.
I blame unpaid bills, the quickness of your sex,
and the stubborn black steeling up your eyes.

But I'm afraid you know
I only love you
when you ride away.

Killing Love on February 14th

The Bladerunner killed his girlfriend today.
He runs on two thin hooks,
lean, muscular, half-metal half-man.
A beautiful new kind of animal.

Today the police cover up burning one of their own.
He was on a murderous rampage American-hero style.
We all know a blaze of glory is the only way to go.

And so, you break up with me on Valentine's Day.
For effect I smash the cake I made you
shatter pieces of chocolate and cheap white china
that's my small blaze.
We text the only words between us
use a series of door slams as periods.

Clearly, this is my fault. You tell me
not to be so nice to you so you can move on.
I don't know how to not be nice without maintaining anger
so I throw things and say fuck a lot.
I'm predatory, only willing to fight after a break.

You tell me I hold all the cards.
I tell you I don't want the cards
Why can't we just be?
Can't you sit still next to me, hold my hand
let me feel this grow up through my rib bones
a green snaking stalk unfolding inside me?

You fail to realize that I live
with a surety that I will disappoint
I don't know how to hit a ball with a paddle,
or how to drink in bars. I'm scared to ride a bicycle,

and sometimes even to leave my own house.
I wanted to learn to be human for you.
I throw the cards back —
you let them fall softly on the floor.

Conversion

I didn't grow up with religion
have only been to church for work and funerals
Having never been much, it's awkward,
I stand not knowing the hymns
stare at the glowing cross
ponder the millions I move through
who adorn themselves with this symbol.

Back lit and menacing, it gives us something to hang on.
Just for a minute, I understand the warmth of the thing
something opens up in me, the need:
for ritual, and belief, for community.
And the pastor makes us laugh, like we belong.

Still, I think his love is conditional
we must love Jesus and put some money on the plate
Hey, I got nothing against Jesus,
I mean, isn't he a hippie kid like me?

But I keep my money in my pocket
and stick to my more practical claim
of spiritual, not religious.
I have to tell you though,
there is a time when Jesus won't stay out of my mouth.

I've never read the bible and the only testifying
I've done is when this man is inside me
suddenly, God and Jesus pour out of me
Oh God, Oh Jesus, Oh Please, Oh God
It's Good

With him I feel faith on my knees
that beatific thing in my mouth

I am fervent-fervid, a zealous believer
Porn plays on the screen, round ass's bounce sacrosanct,
bodies form a cathedral, his skin cocoa-colored, smooth to taste.

He touches me places and I am born again.
I am devotional, his hands on my throat.
He holds himself against my cervix
He's found a space in me no one ever has.

Hallowed be my adoration.
I will return here on my off days,
when his girlfriend and my man are at work
prostrate myself for it, speak in tongues,
catch the spirit, turn myself over to the flesh
in all its ravenous hunger.

The Funny Thing is

I thought about hugging you this morning
how your stocky body fills my arms
and that maybe if I squeezed hard
you'd be okay.

Just okay
just not broken anymore
an aching abandoned boy
bones shifting around unhappily under all that muscle
all that sunshine I used to call your skin
it does light a room.

But maybe that was hunger illuminating your man shell
wiser women would have run
but I wanted to touch it,
feel the warmth of your pliable insides
all those guts your mother twisted up
mixing your batter till your idealism and revulsion for women
was all syrupy like regurgitated Robitussin
burning on the way out, but sweet I mean Damn

Most of us are ridiculous enough to enjoy adoration
we just never understand the price of it.
I was your pop star dirtying my reluctant pedestal
you sticking cameras in my face
tripping me up with questions
and broadcasting my failures all over the place.

I didn't want to be part of your slippery image
one minute your good girl, the next a loose woman.
I see now how you were turned to an object
a babysitter masturbating on you
a mother who threw you away.

I get it how you need to fuck on top
so as not to suffocate. I do too
for the same crushed down reasons.

Cougar in Scrubs

I want to be pawed
try to force him in the bathroom
the smell of shit from the hospital beds around us.
I lick his neck, reach in his pants.

Get no satisfaction manhandling his tiny frame
I must outweigh him by sixty pounds
smash tongue into lips, my bra is too thick,
his arms don't bend right.

I'm whispering in his ear
don't you miss this
I pull his dick to my crotch
wrestle to free nipple to mouth
here at work.

I want him to tell me
he wants me
can't go another day
without tasting me
and although he agrees
he takes no lead.

He is scared
enjoys the chase more than the catch
I can't tell him that I do too,
so much so that if he would only do it
breakdown and swear his devotion
I would be free
free to not like him anymore
lose interest
walk away.

How I Lost the Kitchen Guy

I used to brush against him in the nursing home kitchen
as I filled steaming plastic mugs of coffee for my patients
sweat on my forehead remembering a late night flight to his house
where I kicked and pulled the cushions off the couch
his lips and tongue on my back bending me over
shaking with adrenaline I must have licked his tiny tummy
pulled hard dick from sweatband waist
and devoured him on that couch and floor
while reaching for my chiming trembling phone.

I was late, busted, out-a-bounds
and we worked side by side
afraid to look in each other's eyes
beads up my back I spill coffee
and head through the swinging door
text him about it from the bingo table
we smile but don't talk out loud
while pulling supper trays
our lips come within a half inch
Jo Jo the Pilipino kitchen aide
catches the moment looks away fast
God this fire is eating me whole
say hello to my old mojo.

I fucked it all up
when he started working in housekeeping.
didn't get caught in my lie
but in heat and so alive, I lost my shit
right on instant message couldn't hold it in.
The girls buzzing around pollinating his cute self
holding his broom and dustpan he flirts.
They find work in his assigned rooms.
He lingers at the nurses' station

and I have a fit slide a finger across my throat
thumb type madly break it off
sure he'll recognize my juicy superiority
I play myself.

Now we pass awkwardly in the hall
sparks held in with regret
and my guilt is not from my cheating
but from being unable to restrain
my stupid angry texts.
I thought I could force his hand
want to force them to touch me again.
I check my phone a thousand times a day
want to quit my job, call in sick
the clock crawls.
He pushes laundry baskets by
I push bed scales, look away.

My panties used to stay wet all day
vibrate with his messages.
These days I'm chewing my gum too hard
barely eating, staying up late
looking for someone online, buying more wine
that I want to take to his house mix with Hennessy
taste his cleanness in the shower.
I'm looking for a new secret to keep
to burn my stomach like hot coal
worm its way through me
keep my nipples hard
but it's gone.

I'm an empty glass pipe and I wait.

Lunch with Big

My body is trained to the muffler rumble of his muscle car.
The candied paint, gleaming chrome rims slice air, turn heads.
A gangbanger showpiece it reeked of danger, speed,
thumping bass, and purple berry air freshener.

Riding him knees burning on the armrest
rubbing runs in my stockings down to my toes.
My hands gripping the T-top
suit skirt up around my waist
his massive lips around my tits
everything is in the right place
my knee hurts but it's so good
and then I'm running late.

Back to work hair unraveling
stockings torn and a shit-eating grin.
The phone technician smirking at my desk.
Out of breath I blurt
late lunch
and we both laugh looking down
at my destroyed hose.

Lunch with Big II

He picked me up from the office, brought me a burrito.
We drove to Lake Merritt.
We'd fucked in the parking lot before
steamed up the windows like lots of people do.
But we didn't have sex that day, I just ate my burrito.
I had to get back to work.

On the way back a woman was scowling at us in his rearview.
It's that bitch Debra he said calmly,
his heart had to be thudding like mine.
It was the woman he lived with.

She knew who I was, I knew who she was,
I'd never seen a picture of her,
but she had seen mine while we were on the phone
and she was going through his stuff.
She'd found my number on his cell phone bill when
he was out of town with his ex, cheating on both of us.

Everyday he picked me up from work
took me to get my son, gave me time to cook,
put the baby to bed, then come back.
We'd fuck for hours, every night delicious.
Him showering and leaving by 11 p.m.
when her shift ended at the post office.

She followed us close, mean mugging.
He pulled past my building, stopped to let me out.
She got out of her car.
I couldn't let her think she could intimidate me
or that she could stop me from seeing him.
She said something about me having said I would
so I swung on her.

He jumped in the middle and we tussled around him,
hitting wildly. I kept yelling
Ain't shit changed, ain't shit changed
I wanted her to know he wasn't hers.
She was just the fool who paid his bills.

I got her pretty good with the heel of my pump.
She got back in her car her head bleeding
and asking for an ambulance
I cracked her windshield with the shoe and she
drove off with my other one.

I ran a hand over my wild head, patches of hair torn out,
scratches and broken nails on my hands.
Pounding with adrenaline I walked in stocking feet past security
across the slate floor to the elevators.
No one had noticed the performance outside.

On the 15th floor I slid behind my desk, answered the phone.
Law Offices, voice shaky,
I hit another line, called my friend.
Girl, you're not gonna believe this one

The Audacity of Sparrows

I once heard a woman
play cello in the parking lot
of the mountains where I walk
rising with morning mist off green.

You kissed me slower yesterday
both lips defined eating mine.

Sometimes a guy plays the saxophone
between buildings downtown
the sound bounces around
softens concrete and steel.

Your body was like that yesterday
filled me up, you brought it down
our flab succulent between us
desire climbs like vines
as bold as a little brown bird
stealing from the bowl
of a large brown dog.

Have you ever played with a toy car
the kind you pull back and you pull back
and you set it down
when the tension is built —
it takes off bumping into walls
and table legs, switching directions
without losing momentum?

I'm like that, dear,
when you warm me up.

What If I Can't Wiggle Out of It

With all my tadpole might
I wish I could reverse insemination.
I have been pregnant more that not.
My nipples like glass in your mouth
My insides hungry gravel.
Hard sharp stones
no love, only desire
I just ate but I want more.

I stripped in a dark damp motel with beach sand feet
was torn apart by mouths and entered.
I want a rematch.
The lips and arms I crave don't sleep beside me.
He waits for me. I roll over, give him my back,
check my phone, wish he'd snore so I could masturbate.
My hormones are raging around the fire of my burning womb.
I wish my backyard would prove so fertile.

I need a new season
the Christmas tree lays dead on the sidewalk
I'm tired of cold feet
holding my heat in so you'll understand
I'm leaving you.

This morning I took the pads from my purse
put them back under the sink.
Periods come when you're not prepared
so I wear white panties.
Later I'll feel a slight cramp
hurry to check the tissue
for that slight pink
like a sunrise.

Nothing Planned Nobody's Parenthood

In the waiting room, long faces sandwiched by dreary walls.
Couples sit hunched into each other whispering lament,
mostly wanting to get it over with.

It's an end to a beginning. A relief
from the sickness, exhaustion, and hunger
that comes loaded with fear. The wait is long.
They take you in then send you back to wait.
Many times you waver, stare longingly at the exit.

My man couldn't take it. He said the room and
the whole vibe was making him nauseous.
He hid in the car passing hours.
I stayed waiting for impact.

Death of cells or death of souls
my little bean-shaped child taking up some
grey area on the ultrasound screen. No
wooompa woompa heartbeat or tiny waving hands.
On the table I feel like meat, bloody butcher paper
scrunched under my bare shamed ass.

First we spread our legs, get into trouble.
Then we spread our legs to get out.
The table is stained. Like me, it's seen a lot of traffic.
I say goodbye to a red lump in an emesis basin,
feel all that's shitty
about being human
about being a woman
about having choices and not having options.

I don't know how these doctors do it,
set their teeth and go about the work.

They tell themselves it's lifesaving,
and I'm not saying that it isn't.

I'm just saying I don't think
I'm the only one here
even more afraid
of the dirty feeling than the pain.
Imagining days, miles of regret.
Children that shine like a full moon
like a heat wave in January, pure confusing sunshine.

But back here on planet earth
I'm hurtling along, head fuzzy on the exam table.
The decision has been made and though he says
he doesn't hold it against me, some days
he describes the bare feet on wood sound of first steps.
The way they speed up when they see you.
Little faces held close the scent of milk sweet breath
a tiny flawless you.

And he told me after it was done
that he would have taken the baby everywhere
gotten up every night even if it was all night.
But there is no more baby to wake us.

Without a Roof

This love between us grew up
from under the desk of a speed freak.
It tapes LED lights with black electrical tape
cooks iguana over open fire
tastes sweet like suckling pig.

Sparked by a kiss in FoodsCo parking lot
we rode on jetliners, landed in the same city
moved in a closed curve points on the same plane.
I kept your stories in a red bandana
carried them over my shoulder coast to coast
all these years.

A love born of heartbreak, me tired
from the weight of belongings thrown out the door.
Exhausted from being a good girl to men
who could only see me in the rearview mirror.
And you sat on a curb leaking
the tears wouldn't stop so you walked
away from your job and everything you owned
smoke circling a glass pipe, blood in a syringe.

I spent my inheritance, did a great job playing house
had boyfriends who smoked weed in bed all weekend long
shades drawn, boyfriends who strung me along
I fought with drunks till dawn.

Relationships left me looking for morning
barefoot and alone in my kitchen.
But now you're here and we are
the pot-bellied versions of our young selves.

Only we know these wrinkles are illusion:

I do recall my hands full of your hair,
you can still see me black rimmed eyes,
flight jacket, 32 waist size.
Only we know these love handles, this baldness
is transient too and should be worn like a badge.

Enter the Dragon Lady

My compulsion is the color of this white boy's eyes
'cause I never knew blue like this before
the shy way he talks to me like I'm holding a bottle of his past
the wildness of it, as if I can twist the top off
let him inhale without the bruising fall from the wagon.

I was there, back in the day I knew him,
at least I knew some of our dead friends,
friends who overdosed, who couldn't give up the ghost.
His eyes are astonishing against dark lashes.
He is educated, far from the streets now.
A white boy with the slickness of Tres Flores still in his hair
a savvy and well groomed cholo disguised among the suits.
He lives between worlds as I do
wants to peer into my blackness
without succumbing to the intensity of my gravity
but I'm dangerous.

See, this is my addiction
this charge is what I get high off
the expectation of touch sitting too close
the masses of bodies the distance between
acceleration, free fall
sipping tea from a paper cup outside his office
wiggling my pink come-fuck-me toes.

Our hour is up, he has to go back to an air conditioned office
a computer, proposals to write, meetings to attend,
a lovely wife and child after five. I text him, tell him
you shouldn't, we shouldn't, do anything
He used the word adulterous, and this guy, he's sweet
but I'm going to bully him, throw my size into it the way I do.

I'm feral, on the run, I don't ever want to be in a meeting
in a building with windows that don't open
fifteen stories in the no-air, or married.
I want to bare my wolf teeth to his neck
pull him away just for a bit from the mortgage,
the childcare bill, the cubicle constraint.

I'm just a bad influence and I ask myself
why can't I want to be like him when I grow up,
not just want him, to fuck him in secret,
as if his success and stability will rub off on my skin
as my fleshy ways sticky and sweet will inflame his.

Anatomy of the Locksmith

We met in a dead drunk twenty-some years back,
had sex I don't remember.
I hung my head but you didn't chin lift, you were cool.
Humble is sexy in my book.

You remind me of our old dead friend.
You the one who got sober
him the one that OD'd.
Your body tight stocky like his was against my large frame.
Is it okay that I lean down when I bury my face in your neck?

There was whiskey involved and a blackout when we met —
Was I sixteen or seven? Had I a shaved head or a bob?
But I saw you at the Fairyland when my son was first born.
Me starving in leopard pants, heart broken by a man with
the same initials as yours, you with some trashy looking white girl
toting some other guy's kid.

I didn't know you, didn't remember you inside me,
whether we had kissed or not. Only that I awoke in a bright room
pants down, alone. I didn't like her for you
thought you might belong with me and mine.
Or is that too much to ask a white guy about my black baby?
My baby daddy never had anything much to do with anything
still, maybe it is too much.

Another thirteen years or so and we crossed paths again
I was engaged, a house full of kids and dogs. You looked inviting
something broken I wanted to glue treasure on a high shelf.
But I just hugged and left you in the coffee shop.
You sober folks and your coffee,
us writers destined to cross you with our love of cafes.

When you popped up again
those wide bitable jaw bones
silvering hair spoke to me
whispered in a nonchalant way
and that hug on our goodbye
your eyes betray the wall you've constructed
and I got news for you.
I've already scaled it
I'm good like that
a practiced thief under your skin.

One day you'll realize
I've moved in where soft skin cups water
between your sternum and scapula.
I'll spoon your clavicle, sleep there.

The only long bone to lie horizontal
clavicle   from clavicula
me, your little key.

Highlander

My ol' man Mike comes home from a visit
to county hospital Highland's ER
he calls it the intergalactic portal.
Laughing sadly he says
There were Lord of the Rings characters up in there,
that he wasn't sure if he should help them
or get out a sword and behead them.
He says he felt like Luke Skywalker in the monster bar.

He's talking about dope fiends
around here the devastation is awesome,
the crack plague leaves people
looking like extras on a zombie movie set,
dangling limbs in mismatched designer clothes,
layers of sweat and street, uncombed hair
or what's left of it.

He says he saw what he decided was a level
a little lower than rock bottom
the guy sitting next to him with sole of shoe hanging off,
smell of rotting meat mixed with unwashed funk,
sucked in cheeks over jack o'lantern teeth,
and long burning high beam eyes.

Mike turned to a quiet hipster girl
sitting on his other side and said simply
dope ain't cool.
Surprised at words from a stranger
she answered in a grave voice *no it's not.*
She has some experience with it and so does he.
*Do you think he could ever be normal
if he got clean?* he wonders out loud.
The girl is not sure either.

The girl has been waiting to be seen all day
and when she finally gets up the nerve to ask the nurses why
they tell her she's missed her name
and send her to the back of the line where she quietly cries.

You in the Town

Where our burned brown grass blows with Swisher Sweets
and orange Cheeto bags the kids call *Hot Chips*
beg for them like crackheads searching for rocks.
The comforting rooster's crow
wakes us to helicopters and traffic jams
each murder more terrifying and awful
but the white folks keep coming
each week we spot a new one in our neighborhood
with their bicycles and Smart cars.

The new colonizers
armed with flannel shirts, beards,
too many tattoos, and black framed glasses.
They farm corner lots and keep bees. For this, we are grateful
but the high rents they carry across the bridge with them,
the organic eateries, green bike lanes,
and café tables taking up parking spaces
are bitter blessings.

Tenants find notices on their doors, landlords
praise this second coming in real estate-land.
Farmers' markets sprout up, and not so ironic
art is everywhere. But these idealist kids, they
don't understand the tribulations they peddle into.
The deep east out lands they don't venture in.
They can't grasp the reasons they are walking targets,
find themselves cold muzzle to temple
stripped of all their hip-hipster cash.

They think they're struggling, broke
but have never felt inherited desperation,
the day-in day-out eating of Top Ramen,
lucky to slice hot dogs or dump Hot Chips into salty noodles.

Have never felt the whip of an extension cord on wet skin,
or lived in fear of enemies who only hate them
for looking just like them, fatherless and angry
strapped with frustration and bullets.

So many cold hard guns fill these streets
vegetables help to feed bellies and brains
but with no jobs and education, the divide continues.

These cool kids landing here, thinking
it's the new winterless Brooklyn
will cycle back to suburbia
when they find themselves staring down
that barrel of hunger, flat black eyes,
young, dreadlocked, born of these streets,
born in the struggle.

Five Minutes of Funk

I heard the neat pop of a glass bottle when I backed out tonight
turned the heads of young Latinas at the taco stand.
My radio was beating loud, they were expecting a dude
but got me, busty and blonde.
At the red light I see the riff and raff
that collects by the Black and White market
me being the only white thing around.

Across the street Las Palmas keeps a line
for the worst burritos in town
Chinese people make them for black folks
in a mostly Latino neighborhood.
Traffic at this corner is often held up by those
exchanging phone numbers and today I wasn't even mad
at the green light, the girl being so cute I could see why
the youngster I was stuck behind
was willing to miss the light for her sunglasses and lip gloss.

The game in the ghetto is one of pulling someone else's catch
looking for a renegade.
All kinds of ulterior motives, broke-ness and broken-ness.
the hustle gassing the hunt.

The prey, head wrapped and pajama panted by day
come night on East 14th you'll see hooker scenes
you thought only existed in the movies,
so many stilettos clacking and ass crammed in skin tight.

You will discover the only economy
that's not suffering is this economy.

Outside El Gato Negro Pool Hall

I drive that way on purpose
to watch the girls
prostitutes young and shiny
shimmering tight dresses
lip gloss glint in streetlight glow
rump roast asses on display like rotisserie
more sexy to me more real than club girls
the way they strut that dark corner
between a Vietnamese croissant factory
and a mental health facility
I once applied to work at.

The day I went to the interview,
I tried to get in through an employee entrance
walked the gauntlet of parking lot
weed smoking wig wearing women
too much plucking of the eyebrows
and loud acrylic on their Frito Lay nails.

I was at the wrong building
it took three tries to get buzzed in to the right one
where the Pilipino nurses tried to stifle
their laughter at a perky white girl
(that's my interview face)
applying to work behind razor wire
in this brown walled cement block of a place
as an underpaid Nurse Aide.

Neighbors

The daughter was a prostitute when she could get work.
A crackhead mostly with hair extensions hanging
all the way to her ravaged ass.
Eyes buck, skin black, teeth missing,
A grinning lipsticked clown who sang along the train tracks.

She often flew into rages at her mother.
When the door was locked she'd break out all the windows.
From the triangle glass in the house's peak
which flooded our little cribs with light
our own little triangle of sky —
some people covered theirs with foil
while I invited every inch inside.
They didn't want sunshine to interfere with their TVs.

She'd break out the picture window below
which still didn't gain her entry.
Our windows were barred from the inside,
a weird aesthetic that, with cute curtains and time,
you could get used to.
On the outside it was meant to look less like a fortress.
Even though we lived in Housing they told us when moving in
You're rich compared to the people across the tracks.

She'd break the kitchen window above the little triangle sink,
cussing at her mother the bitch
who I guessed from my exhausted bed
must have dope or money she didn't want to share.
Lying awake I imagined the glass of my sleeping son's window
shattering on his bed the possibility of gunshots
following words through his walls.
I'd tiptoe into his room slide his heavy body
out of bed across the hall to mine.

The family next door was large: some days I came home
to see a handful of handicapped people smiling moon faces
at nothing from a blanket on the lawn. Some of them were white,
the only other whites I'd seen out here
where PG&E might not fix your lights for days,
where getting a package left on your doorstep could be daunting.

There was an auntie-lady so super-crazy
she'd shaved her whole head except for
one long braid hanging from the top
as if waiting to pull her up out of there.
She sat in a plastic chair by the door clapping her hands loudly,
shouted profanities, threats, and rants at us.
Once she rang my doorbell, asked for a knife
I politely told her that I didn't have any.

A grandson stayed there for a spell:
He'd wave enthusiastically when I walked to the mailbox
from a window that could only have been in the bathtub.
I felt a little sorry for him, stunted and slow,
I took him to the park with us.
He told me he'd never been across the water to San Francisco
he never even imagined going a few blocks to the train
getting a couple dollars together
to see one of the most beautiful cities in the world.
I drove there everyday.

After the park I brushed him off, scared he'd try to follow me in
heard him once through the wall, say something
worse than *Fuck you, Grandma.*
The ugliest words I've ever heard.

Eventually the family was evicted and another moved in.
The guy was a junk man, a real Fred Sanford
with a truck full of junk.
Anything I put on the lawn he carted off.
His women looked like a troll, short and round with bug eyes
staring in two different directions.

She rang my bell at all hours, called me a name that wasn't mine
asked me for ice and steel wool.
I heard him beating her sometimes,
the hollering and breaking sounds.
The shuffling of someone living in the shed
attached to the back of my house.
And once I looked out my back window
he'd put a whole trailer home right there in Housing Authority
under the pine trees between the train track's
iron triangle.

My White Flight

On his way to the store
a white van stops beside my boyfriend
the back door opens, an automatic weapon pointed
he raises his arms, looks to the sky
a voice from the front seat says it's not him
he opens his eyes, the van is gone.

My wings are itching now
and I think how I used to love
sinking into the sprawled badness of this town
it's such a mess I can slide through unnoticed
among the other misfits and outlaws.

But lately the news in Oakland makes me cry
three-year-olds are shot off their tricycles,
run over crossing the street, a man is murdered
while feeding the homeless with his daughter,
a man is murdered at the ATM in front of his son.

Writers like me in coffee shops robbed of laptops
shot for resisting. And I think I'd stay if the ghetto
was only on the outside of my spiked metal gate
but the problem is it's on the inside too
and it's not the good kind of ghetto
the soul full of music, bubbling pots of greens
on a back burner, corner philosophers,
foiled plates from taco trucks and barbeques.

It's the bitter-hater kind
the selfish piss on your doorstep,
throw your trash on the ground kind.
The drink the last drop of Kool-Aid
and leave an empty pitcher
taunting the rest of us kind.

The Raptor on E. 14th

There's a tower in East Oakland.
Down by Seminary on the hoe stroll, that's where he lives.
I've never seen him but I heard from the air conditioning guy.
He hunts this wasted tundra of coke smokers, winos,
Baby girls on colt legs wobbling by on stilettos
thick-assed mini-skirted vets holding up street corners.

Like the girls, the Great White Owl uses
the sit and wait style of hunting.
His penthouse home is high in the brick tower
above the low-standing blighted buildings of the flat lands.
Above the taco trucks and ice cream carts of the surenos.
He's built a queen-size nest surrounded by shit pellets
and pigeon carcasses like fried chicken bones
outside The Fish King a few blocks up.

I want to stalk this bird of prey
catch him in action
taloned king of the ghetto
he rules among scavengers
no one scraping up much more
than a welfare check or a stolen flat screen.

Saying Sorry to Cats by Moonlight

This moon has followed me since I was a child in the back seat
standing on my knees, face to the window.
It holds a bunny, an Easter bunny, a Peter Cottontail,
a Thumper bunny like the one I had in a wire cage
till the dogs got a hold of him
and tore him to pieces in the driveway.
Mom yelling out the bathroom window for me to turn away,
look away, but it was too late I saw his pink insides stretched long
and elastic between their mouths. Dogs are rotten that way.

Mine woke me, before the full moon when the night was still black,
last week a scuffle on the back porch and I ran out there
blindly hitting at furred bodies then ran backwards to find the light
Rosie had a cat wrapped around her neck like a muffler
a beautiful calico with fur of delicate grey and brown.
I hit Rosie with a spatula until it broke in two
the cat ejected itself and you grabbed Chopper
who was rushing forward with his great big jaws.
But the cat made it off under the trellis
We saved it, we said, congratulating ourselves
and scolding the cat killers. We saved that cat's life.

But yesterday I looked in my garden
pissed the dogs had dug another hole
my nasturtium and morning glory seeds all upended
the futility of it all had me feeling upended as well
in the pile of dirt, she was buried.
The dogs knew they were wrong.
They had captured the cat and planted her
frozen in clawed flight
in my flowerbed under a full moon.

116

The Rooster on Two-Six

Recently on my return from work
a rangy group of kids was running the neighborhood
looking for their lost rooster.

Later I heard an upset of wings
and dog snarls from behind the house
and knew my pit bulls had a hold of him.
From the look of their feathered mouths
I thought for sure he was a goner.
I called in the dogs, leaving a trail
of feathers and muffled squawks.

But I'll be damned if 24 hours later
after the third time we called the dogs off
he limp walked right out our front gate
and disappeared into someone else's yard.

Now every morning in the early hours
I hear crowing and feel proud,
think of the Chinatown gold medallion
I used to wear on my neck.

Year of the rooster,
and I'm glad to be one
cause that was some badass cock
walking away from a dog fight.

Birders

This morning a bluebird was trapped in my kitchen
I held her fragile body, panicked wings
afraid they'd turn to powder like a moth's
I ran, dog at my heels, to the rosemary bush
and threw her up where she flew away.

Last night on my birthday
there was a drive-by out front.
A carload of death lit up our street.

And I can't decide if it's time to change everything
or if I've really made it home.
To this place full of contradictions
here in the Murder Dubs, the middle east of Oakland
with my rosebushes and sparrows.

Where my best friend is a little brown dog
just as fearful and ferocious as me, growling
at everyone who comes too close to our gate,
when outside it she cowers
from passing trucks and loud noises.

At night while I sleep under my purple comforter,
she stalks the fence, hunts trespassers and small animals.
During the day I confront the world, wrestling from it
things I need, retreat tired feet through our peeling blue door.
She waits head on my pillow, muddy feet
tucked in to my clean sheets.

Death in the Beer Garden

I bought a Tiger Lily at the grocery store
planted it in my back yard
with it memories of how they grow wild in Vermont,
how my mother planted them wherever she lived,
and how their freckles look just like
those of sun-kissed girls.

The snails ate the petals off, the leaves off,
each day less lily until only a sad stalk remained.

Angry at the assault I throw a whole box of salt
trying to kill the bastards in their cute swirl of shell.
I discover thousands of them like barnacles
on the underside of lawn chairs,
Eating holes through my roses and the lemon tree.
They converge on the candles I leave burning
a whole snail party wiggling and warming its antennae.

Salty with me now, they leave shiny silver trails
on every inch of every thing in the yard
I try organic snail poison, then remember
Mom told me to pour them cups of beer.

As it turns out, snails are lushes.
They crowd the beer that leaves them dead
concentration cups full of paper-soft shells.
With a gloved hand I crush them,
vengefully use them to fertilize my plants.
Now the plants they no longer feast on,
can feast on them.

Spring Fever

Every day a white van drives slowly down our street
The driver squeezes a bicycle horn and hollers
Tamales, Pollo, Elote, Tamales,
It's music that makes your stomach rumble.

The wind here blows orange Cheeto bags like fall leaves,
blunt, and Trojan wrappers into my driveway.
When I pull in the compost can,
I smile at the misplaced foil and plates from down the street.

The neighbors have set up a taco stand on the sidewalk.
From Friday afternoon till Sunday night they grill meat
chop it, and serve it on tortillas
with radish and jalapeno on the side.

These things cause me tiny pieces of joy
as does the bird riot in the bush weeds out back.
A ridiculous around the clock cacophony
that must be mating or an abundance of good berries.

I leave the windows open on a warm night.
Pornos play loudly with my moaning and the frantic bird song.
We drink alcohol flavored with ice tea and Jolly Ranchers.

And can't stop laughing at this one bossy porn guy
who keeps telling the girl in doggy style to
arch it out, arch it out
Unsatisfied in the way she lifts her ass to him
though he didn't even take the time
to remove his ugly black tennis shoes.

The Language of Rice Farmers

Sitting in the back yard
thinking about earthquakes,
Katrina, and zombie apocalypse.
I plan to retrofit and reinforce.
Someday I'll start my urban farm
get some solar panels but I'm distracted
by a bird that thinks it's a DJ
mixing and scratching the same tune for hours.
Another sounds a lot like a car alarm.
I hear the cock's crow, his hen's clucking.
A SkillSaw squeals of new things built.
The rattling trunk of a bass-filled scraper
competing with the Mariachi's oompa loompa sound.
An argument turns to the sharp pap pap of gun fire.

On our street there are pigeons and chickens
eating Top Ramen together, dodging the
latest rotation of thrown-away Chihuahua mutts
zippering in and out of double parked cars and speed bumps.
The Chinese lady picking through our trash
wears a polyester suit and a sombrero.

My neighbors carry in a bloody quartered pig.
They look guilty, as if it's a human corpse.
I smile back because I love them:
a chain-smoking gang of young Nepali men
bounce and giggle around the front porch night and day
the women come and go, squat on their haunches
brushing long hair and clutching cell phones
they wait for shared rides to work while the men play.

Spicy smells come from their back yard,
where rows of marigold bushes bejewel

the bottle recycling operation that makes a clinking music
long past dark. Once a month someone borrows a truck
and the whole thing is overflowing with dog food bags
full of bottles and cans.

Listen to me and the dogs growl
happily wiggle bare feet in the half-dead
East Oakland grass.

Mooning Over You, Boo

Nights like these we see the same full moon
yours between six palm trees
waving silver in two neat rows
a neighborhood I have no hope of affording
feel too noisy and large for
when I speed through in my bass-heavy ride.

My moon smiles yellow between buildings
subsidized and working class at best.
Here in the flatlands we wake to the smash and grab
sidewalk diamonds, rear window glass,
gunfire pop and helicopter hover.

But, hey, this is where I am,
and when I sit in the back
with the birds and my dogs
I don't aspire to much more.

I get how quiet it is at your place,
how we can sleep with the door open
and every little catfight
brings a head from a manicured door.

The moon understands
these are just neighborhoods
places where we sleep.

The moon sees us for the young fools we still are.
Sure, we have the trappings of adulthood
the responsible steel toe boots you kick around in,
my bluff-talk of mortgages and good school districts.

The moon knows we are still those kids

the scared ones, boning under whiskey's influence.
Not really knowing why we go through the act
strangers in our own skin
pressing costumed bodies together
leather jackets and flights
coats that come with identity, or so we hope.
And this goes on into the moonlight of our forties
scared to death of just asking for what we want.

Spirit in the Dark

I spent Saturday night playing songs on YouTube
Sunday morning songs in the car
I've blown a speaker leaving a sad cheap growl
where the bass ought to be.

The songs I replay sing to tears
modern versions of those that rose from fields
sprouting wings soaring off
over the big house
over the Atlantic
call it heaven
call it home.

The intangible moment
when the one you desire
desires you
meets you in cottony skies
naked but for your wings
wet pearls
a first kiss on top of the rollercoaster.

One bright morning
when this life is over
I'll fly away.

Acknowledgments

Grateful acknowledgment is made to the editors of the following publications where some of these poems first appeared in slightly different formats:

Criminal Class Review, Enizigam, Unlikely Stories, Gloom Cupboard, Opium Poetry, Rusty Truck, Zygote In My Coffee, Underground Voices, The Legendary, Riverbabble, Napalm and Novocain, Black Listed Magazine, Visceral Uterus, The Weekenders, Zombie Logic Review, Pink Litter, Lit Up Magazine, Citizens For Decent Literature, Bicycle Review, Tres Corazones, Dead Snakes, Out of Our, Zero Percent Magazine, Sparkle and Blink, Horror Sleaze Trash, Rolling Thunder Press, Regardless of Authority

About the Author

Cassandra Dallett occupies Oakland, California. Cassandra writes of a counterculture childhood in Vermont and her ongoing adolescence in the San Francisco Bay Area. She is widely published online and in print magazines. Her work has appeared in *Slip Stream, Sparkle and Blink, Hip Mama, Bleed Me A River, Criminal Class Review,* and *Out of Our* among many other publications.   www.cassandradallett.com